The Essence
RELAXATI

GW01463961

The Essence of
RELAXATION

Compiled by:
VANDANA

Crest Publishing House

(A JAICO ENTERPRISE)
G-2, 16 Ansari Road, Darya Ganj
New Delhi - 110 002

THE ESSENCE OF RELAXATION
ISBN 81-242-0137-4

First Edition : 1998
Reprinted : 2003

Published by:
CREST PUBLISHING HOUSE
(A Jaico Enterprise)
G-2, 16 Ansari Road, Darya Ganj
New Delhi-110002

Printed by:
Gayatri offset Press
A-66, Sector-2, NOIDA-201301

INTRODUCTION

We live in a time where everyone has to go through a lot of stress and tension. To live a happy and normal life one has to know how to relax so that one is always at the peak of physical ease and mental peace. This book gives you a glimpse of how to lead a tension-free life with the art of relaxation.

Relaxation is not just recreation or getting away from one's daily routine. It is more than just that. In fact, sometimes recreational activities where physical and mental works are involved tend to make a person more tired. This book talks about how to unwind oneself without getting away from one's daily routine.

Being relaxed means to be at ease with your work, your duties, your obligations and most important of all, your physical and mental abilities. Through relaxation you not only avoid the stresses and tensions in life but also become more productive and confident.

The first and probably the most important step towards relaxation is to avoid tension. You need not be an escapist to avoid tension. That is, you don't have to shy away from anything, just identify your sources of tension and learn to cope with them.

If you clearly know what problem is currently bugging you, you will immediately know the source of your tension.

❄❄❄

Try to set the problem right. There is not a single common life situation with which you cannot cope.

At the same time, while trying to cope with a problem, don't try to fight it. Instead take the problem in your stride. If the place where you are reading this book is a bit dark, light up a lamp. This will immediately make you feel relaxed.

Another very important thing in our daily life is to learn to slow down. We live in fast times when everything around us moves at a breathtaking pace. Our body and mind are not made to take this pace. We must take our breaks so that we do not get over-exhausted.

We tend to expect too much from ourselves as well as from others. It is better not to do so. To avoid breakdowns and burn-outs taking definite periods of complete, deliberate and controlled rest is a must. Never, never compromise on rest.

We generally have a psycho-physical control in-built within our system which takes care of our general feeling of well-being.

※ ※ ※

The key to relaxation is to keep our natural controls in tune.

Stresses in one's natural controls may happen due to various factors: fatigue, excessive eating or drinking, dehydration, poor blood circulation, adverse environmental conditions like heat, cold or pollution and faulty basic attitude about yourself and others.

One of the easy ways to tune back the normal controls is to get into that corner of your home where you feel most relaxed. It may be the library or in front of your TV set or simply sitting and doing nothing on your favourite rocking chair.

It helps to have proper air-circulation while you are relaxing at your favourite corner. Fresh air is always good for health. But mind you, don't turn this advice into a fetish -- you may develop bronchial problems if the air outside is too cold!

Have you ever thought of the colours on the walls at home? If it is not possible to change the entire decor, at least try and change the shades on walls of your favourite spot. Pastel shades of blue, green, grey and pearl are usually most soothing to the nerves.

Who doesn't know that music plays a very important role on one's mind? Choice of music is usually very subjective, but soothing music which usually blends in the background without being distracting is very helpful to lift one's mood.

Have you noticed how cats and dogs at home do a kind of muscle-stretching and wriggling? They do so to relax and we can also do the same. Regular stretching exercise not only makes you feel happy but it tones up your muscles too. Result: you become a more confident person.

Have you noticed that people tend to yawn when they are tired or sleepy? Actually yawning helps restore oxygen supply to your brain and makes you feel relaxed. Never supress a yawn unless you are in a situation where it is socially rude to yawn.

Set some time for relaxation alone. Let all your muscles relax to the point when the entire body feels limp. Mentally you feel at ease and reach a point where the mind is blank. There is a difference between sleeping and relaxing and pure relaxation can sometimes be more rejuvinating than sleep.

Physically, our eyes tend to get stressed faster. The eyes not only reflect our emotions, but also mirror our state of health and general well-being. A daily routine of exercising the eyes -- a chart you can always pick up from a eye-specialist's chamber -- helps one to remain relaxed.

Smiling also helps to keep you relaxed. Smiling relaxes the facial muscles. It also develops a sense of being at-ease with life. Besides, smiling creates a positive impact on people around you and that helps boost your morale.

As most of the time while at work we are sitting, our muscles need periodic relaxation. Learn how to relax while sitting. If you are working with a computer, take away your eyes from the screen after every few minutes. While driving relax at the red lights.

Maintaining a good posture while sitting is very important. Our spinal cord is designed to evenly carry the entire weight of our body. This can be done by sitting straight and avoiding excessive leaning forward or backward.

While standing too maintain a good posture. Adopt the straight-spinal-cord formula and balance the weight of your body evenly on two feet. Good posture not only relaxes your muscles it also makes you feel confident.

A bad posture quite often breeds trouble in body and mind. Your eyes become listless and that adds strain. Excessive drooping can even cause problems of breathing. A bad posture is almost always the main reason for recurring backaches.

A bad posture also indicates that you are depressed. Be concious about your posture when you are depressed. If you can maintain a good posture during a depressing period that can even become a cure for your depression.

Maintain a good posture while walking. Walking is considered the most easy, healthful and natural exercise of the body and mind.

❋ ❋ ❋

Always wear a comfortable footwear while walking briskly.

It is very important to replenish your energy through proper diet. Also there should be periodic checkups with your doctor to ensure proper functioning of body organs. Minor irritations are usually results of improper diets and malfunctioning of one or more organs.

You should develop a daily regimen which should neither be too difficult to follow nor too relaxed so that your body functions do not get a chance to be tuned. Develop your schedule in such a way so that your body and mind are taken care of within the routine.

Deep breathing will always help you relax. In fact, a person's breathing becomes shallow when he is depressed.

✳ ✳ ✳

Develop the habit of breathing rhythmically and deeply always. This will keep your nerves in control and deter depression.

As told earlier, fresh air is very important for a general good health. Open windows of your home at periodic intervals to let in fresh air.

❋ ❋ ❋

Stale air not only restricts oxygen supply to your body, it also breeds mental staleness.

Food habit is very important to keep the body and mind healthy. Avoid too much of junk food and rely more on natural food. Your diet should be balanced and contain all the nutritional ingredients. In case of confusion consult your doctor.

Avoid too much of spicy food. But go by the proverb that variety is the spice of life. Vary your food regularly so that you don't get bored to eat.

❊ ❊ ❊

Mind that it is not the quantity of food that matters -- what is really important is quality food.

Learn enjoying your meals. The more you enjoy eating the more you will increase your digestive power and this will add the necessary nutrients to your body system. Your digestive system should be in good order. Eat plenty of green vegetables to avoid constipation.

Drink plenty of water. In typical Indian climate it helps to drink about ten to twelve glasses of water everyday. Remember your body consists of sixty-six per cent of water. Drinking water not only keeps the balance of fluid in your body, it also checks dehydration and helps the body get rid of harmful toxins.

Always pay attention to the health of your feet. Many people neglect the feet and this creates plenty of problems.

❋❋❋

Remember the feet have many nerve-endings and keeping the feet in good order is very important.

A little bit of physical exercise everyday helps. We are not talking about making you a he-man of sorts, but a daily regimen of moving the muscles through exercise helps get rid of muscle-strains while at work.

Remember physical exercise helps you tone up emotionally too. The excess glandular energy generated by strong emotions like fear and anger as well as strong erotic urges are taken care of by exercise and you tend to become emotionally more stable.

Have you ever noticed how relaxed you become after taking a wonderful bath? It's advisable not to skip baths. Be comfortable while taking a bath -- use the right temperature of water -- and never be miserly in using colognes and deodorants.

An average human being needs between seven and nine hours of sleep daily. Sleep is one of the greatest cure of fatigue and restorer of energy. Your health may not suffer if you don't get your quota of sleep occasionally but never go without sleep in long stretches.

If you are emotionally distressed, your face will show it. Conversely, if you can keep your face fresh you can avoid emotional stress. Applying a cold towel on your face followed by a hot towel and alternating it several times help reduce tiredness.

It is often said laughter is the best medicine. Sure enough, it is. Try to put up a smile on your face even when the going is tough, this will definitely cheer up your soul.

❋ ❋ ❋

It's difficult, but learn to laugh at yourself.

Quietude is very important to lead a tension-free, relaxed life. In present day circumstances, when there is plenty of sound around it helps to set some time to yourself when you live in quiet. Quietude helps recuperate your energy to a great extent.

Whenever you are facing some problem, think about a pleasant situation in life. A soothing effect to your mental unease can be obtained by recalling some particularly pleasant scene in your life or a happy incident during your childhood.

If you have difficulty in recalling a particularly happy memory, try this out: play a happy melody in your music system. Everybody has some happy memory associated with certain music and melody. Treasure them and play them whenever you feel blue.

Meditation is also a good method of relaxation. Meditation helps you to concentrate on your inner self, which, in its turn helps you to understand yourself better. The more you understand yourself the more you know how to relax.

Some people use the method of auto-suggestion to ward off tension effectively. Whenever you have a problem repeatedly tell yourself that nothing has happened, everything will be alright soon. This way you can overcome unnecessary tension in life.

In fact, if you are realistic, you can even be a great achiever by employing the auto-suggestion method. You know what you can achieve in life and go on suggesting to yourself that you *can* do what you want. Say "I will" and this should help you relax.

Verbal repitition is a sure-shot way of auto-suggestion. Go on repeating a particular idea to yourself till you feel comfortable with it. After you have done so, you will feel reasonably relaxed with the idea.

If you think yourself to be incompetent and unworthy, you tend to become so. On the other hand, recognize your potential and possibilities. This will not only help in your auto-suggestion methods, but also make you feel at ease with yourself.

The strongest and single most important thing that holds oneself from complete relaxation is fear. To be fearful of a genuine problem is understandable, but many people are apprehensive of imaginary dangers. Avoid this like plague.

Like fear, anger also has a negative impact on one's personality.

***

Avoid sudden outbursts of anger.

***

Be cool and confident and try to be in control of the situation and your temper.

One of the best ways to control anger is going by the age-old saying: "Count ten before you act in anger." You may have to count ten several times if you are *really* angry. Simply do so till your anger subsides and you feel sufficiently relaxed.

"Don't worry, be happy" is a common line these days. Stick to this slogan. Actually there is no point in worrying about things over which you have no control. Things which you can control yourself should not give rise to any sort of worry, right?

Most people who tend to worry about everything take themselves too seriously.

❀ ❀ ❀

You don't have to do so. Forget the 'I' in you and this will reduce your worries.

Sometimes problems of decision making make a person worry. Whenever in such a situation don't dither. Take a decision this way or the other and then relax. Never mind if you have taken a wrong decision in the process.

It sounds weird, but sometimes physical irritation can be overcome by limpness. When in a dentist's chamber don't get irritated. Instead let your body go limp. You won't feel the pain even if you lose a tooth.

A few simple tricks of relaxation will help you avoid illness. You can avoid digestive problems if you relax for a while before your meals. It's always advisable to eat when you are relaxed rather than when your nerves are taut.

Discord in the family often breeds mental illness. Try to avoid bitterness in the family. In case of an argument in the family remain in the sidelines for sometime, even meditate in the other room till you feel sufficiently relaxed to take part in the argument.

Sometimes excessive elation, that is exuberence, tells on one's mental health. In the event of a major success in life, take success coolly.

❋❋❋

Always let success sink in for a while before you start a celebration.

In modern days depression is probably your worst enemy. There will be times in your life when you'll feel depressed. Some people often need medical help to combat depression. Don't let things to go to that extent. A few tricks can save you from acute depressions in life.

Never take depressions too seriously. Try to understand that depression is somewhat like the weather -- even a very bad day will come to an end. You know that depression will be over and you will be alright.

Never allow mood swings affect your daily routine. Don't let your work remain unfinished.

❋❋❋

Concentrate more on your work and as you get involved in your work, depression takes a backseat.

Don't let self-pity engulf you. Remember there are plenty of people around who are in a worse situation than you. If possible, help them.

❊ ❊ ❊

Social work is a great curer of depression.

Try to analyse what caused your depression. It helps to write down the points which you think made you feel depressed. Once you know why you feel depressed and see them in writing, you know that they are not serious enough incidents to affect your life anyway.

Some people prefer to sleep away depression. If you belong to that lucky group which doesn't have a problem of insomnia, relax and go to bed. Stretch your muscles a bit, put on a soothing music, watch television and after a while you will overcome your blues.

People who get depressed easily usually have a sleep-related problem. Unless it is due to some illness, sleeplessness or insomnia is a hang-over of the modern-day stresses that everyone has to undergo in a civilized society. But relax, there are ways to tackle this problem too.

Check out if you are particularly edgy while retiring to bed. Are your mind too full of thoughts about unfinished work? If that is so go and finish your work or make a plan about it. A few hours of delay in sleep do not affect one's health. So relax!

Your sleeping arrangement should be as free from discomfort as possible. Check out if your blanket is too heavy or too light. Is your bedroom too cold? Is the bed too hard? Remove these discomforts and feel at ease.

A bath before going to sleep helps inducing sleep. But remember that the bath should be soothing and satisfying. A soothing bath helps relax your nerves and you feel sufficiently eager and relaxed to fall asleep.

Your sleeping position should be comfortable. If you enjoy sleeping on your left side, do so. If you prefer right, go ahead. Some doctors advise not to sleep on your back as it might cause snoring. But what's the problem if you are snoring anyway?

Even after all these if you fail to fall asleep after lying in bed for more than half-an-hour, try out a glass of lukewarm milk.

✳ ✳ ✳

Warm milk is a time-tested sedative and also very healthy for your bones.

The proverbial counting of sheep often helps inducing sleep. While counting the sheep you can also take note of their colours and try figuring out what quality of wool can be made from each one of them.

Remember we cannot force ourselves to sleep. Don't try too hard to fall asleep. If sleep is eluding you, never mind. Take up the unfinished letter which you promised to write to your friend. If you have a science background, why not try out a difficult problem from your son's arithmetic book?

THE ESSENCE OF RELAXATION

Try to figure out what are the thoughts in your mind which are hindering your sleep. Obliterate the unpleasant thoughts and worries. Consolidate all the joys you have had during the day. This approach quietens your mind and makes you sleep with a smile on your face.

Indian philosophy is basically about under-standing one's own self.

❊ ❊ ❊

Self-understanding helps to know your basic attitudes and will teach you to appreciate your strengths and recognize your weaknesses.

Many a time irritations in daily life are caused by self-contradictory thoughts.

❊ ❊ ❊

If you develop your self-understanding you should be able to remove these irritations.

Do you have a friend who lends his shoulder to cry? If you are lucky to have a friend like this go ahead and disclose to him your innermost thoughts which are disturbing you.

❄❄❄

Confession is a great relief.

During a period of emotional turmoil, try out writing your diary. Confused thoughts tend to become clearer when you are trying to put them down in writing. You need not be a great writer and it's not necessary to be sensible, reasonable or practical while writing.

If you are particularly bugged about having hurt someone try to analyse to yourself why you have done so. Very rarely an act of inflicting hurt on someone else is unintentional. You may not know, but usually there is a psychological reason behind it.

Some people are essentially ruled by intelligence, while in others emotion play the dominant role. You self-analysis must be able to figure out whether you are dominated by head or heart. Try to strike a balance.

Honesty is the basis of anything you do in life. Be honest while doing the exercise of self-analysis.

✳✳✳

Unless you are true to yourself, you will never be able to understand yourself.

Through a proper self-understanding you will come to know that many a time it's you who is at fault.

❄ ❄ ❄

You stop blaming others for the miseries in your life and thereby become more relaxed.

After a proper and careful self-introspection build on your self-esteem. We often tend to devalue ourselves and this is often the root cause of all problems in life. You will be able to relax more if you are confident in your approach.

Accept yourself as you are. There is no point in thinking that whatever you do will be perfect.

❊❊❊

Everyone errs at time and you can't be an exception. The same rule applies for others.

If you have attained the necessary maturity to face life through proper self-analysis you should be able to win friends. Friends are always a great help in life. Remember that more you increase your capacity for liking others, the happier you are.

Don't be bothered if you feel insecure or shy or embarrassed while talking to a person with whom you want to make friends. The chances are that he too feels the same way. So go ahead with a firm handshake.

Here is a trick for making friends. Never presuppose that the person whom you want to approach will be hostile. Think positively and expect a friendly gesture from him. If you expect hostility you are likely to confront it.

Do you know how to relax on the job? If you don't, the chances are that you think life to be a gloomy affair.

❋ ❋ ❋

While working allow intermittent rest periods and freshen up once in a while. Don't miss the coffee breaks.

Actually it's not very difficult to relax while working. Learn the most practical and easiest way of doing your job. Effect slight changes in position once in a while. Stretch your muscles and go for a walk down the corridor.

Many of us burn out excess mental energy than required while working. Work in the normal pace that suits you most.

Never try to hurry things up -- you are likely to mess up more. Remember: slow but steady wins the race.

If you enjoy your work you should be able to relax while working. But often we do not enjoy the work.

Try to analyse why this is so. Are you bored with your work? Do you dislike the work you are doing?

One of the time-tested methods to avoid boredom in workplace is to watch the colleagues in action.

❋❋❋

Keep your sense of humour handy and engage in friendly, neighbourly contact with them.

Don't have a low self-esteem while you are working.

❋ ❋ ❋

Always remember whatever you are doing has some worth somewhere, otherwise the company would not have hired you.

If you are utterly bored with work simply carry on with it because it's a duty you have to perform to earn your daily bread. It's true that sometimes great poets have to work as clerks and you can't do anything about it. Take work as a routine job but carry on with your other interests when you are out of office.

There are some tricks to relax even when you are playing. Some people take hobbies very seriously and try to be perfectionist even there.

❅ ❅ ❅

Take your hobbies as fun and a playful exercise, don't turn them into obsessions.

Some people like gardening, some would like to go for a swim. Others prefer making model aeroplanes or cars sitting at home.

Be absolutely relaxed in whatever you do. You need not bother if your aeroplane remains half-finished for days.

Painting used to be one of the most satisfying indoor hobbies till recently. Nowadays many people find solace in a home computer. If you can afford one, go for a multi-media PC. An Internet connection is also a great reliever of tension.

Don't ever get involved in a hobby which bores you. Also try to avoid playing games with people who take defeats in friendly games seriously. There is no point in playing a game of cards with someone who behaves like a serious gambler.

If you are not the kind who is entertained by any hobby get involved in some organization. Helping those who are less fortunate than you is always satisfying and deeply stimulating. You can even try joining a political party -- who knows you might make it big in politics!

Why not do something that others hesitate to do? Climbing Mount Everest might be difficult, but maybe you would like the experience of a mountain trek. Or maybe an experience of skiing in snow? What about river rafting?

City driving is one of the most horrid experiences that all of us have to face these days. You have to be reasonably alert while driving and many people drain all energy while doing so. Relax, there are ways to avoid tension in driving.

If you are the nervous kind, driving is not exactly for you. Avoid driving altogether and do some backseat-driving instead. Or maybe you should rely on the city bus service. Remember, by using the city bus service you are doing a great service to the nation by not wasting its petroleum reserve!

If you *have* to travel by your own car, then try to analyse the fellow-drivers on the road. Remember not everyone has read this book and there is always the human error factor in driving. Let others have their way and you should be relaxed and peaceful. You are not in a racing track.

Some people create problems at home by going for a high level of efficiency in running household chores.

Cleanliness and efficiency are needed in running a house but that should never be made into an obsession.

Home is the place where you should 'feel at home'. Never apply the disciplines that you have to follow at your workplace. It helps to sort out work between spouses in a democratic manner rather than having the 'I am the boss' attitude.

Without developing a fetish for cleanliness arrange the household articles in such a way that you don't find anything missing.

※ ※ ※

Misplacing important objects is often the cause of flayed tempers.

Once in a while change the furniture setting in your house. Rearranging household furniture always gives mental relief and rejuvinates a home. Once in a while go for changing furniture. Never buy a furniture merely on the basis of its looks, always see to it that the furniture is comfortable.

Home is never a home unless there is some amount of privacy, some 'space' for you. It is always preferrable to have a room of your own, which gets separated from the house as soon as you shut the door. If this is impossible, earmark a space in one corner of the house as your own where you can enjoy complete privacy.

Genetically we are prone to develop irritation and illness if we are exposed to too much noise. A relaxed home should be as soundproof as possible. Sound can be reduced at home by going in for heavy carpets on the floor and walls. Jute fabric also tends to absorb sound.

Like a comfortable home a good family goes a long way in defining one's attitude. In a happy family none of the members is overbearing on the other. No one acts to make the husband or the wife feel weak, dependent or too important. In a relaxed home performing normal duties give immense pleasure.

If behaviour of someone in your family annoys you, never be resentful or revengeful in your attitude. Help the person in overcoming his or her behaviour. Remember you can only make matters worse by being resentful.

No one can have a personal life free from all problems and difficulties. Like in your work, try sorting out the problems. If the family members are receptive, a meaningful discussion always helps to solve problems. Never run away from problems at home.

A reasonable control over one's emotions helps overcome the problems in the family. But at the same time see to it that your emotional control is not interpreted as your lack of interest or concern for the others.

Be realistic with family members. Where there is love there is bound to be some hate. You would only hate a person if you feel for for him or her.

❅ ❅ ❅

However, never allow hatred to take over any relationship.

Being a housewife is probably the most difficult part to play in a household. If you are only a housewife, relax and enjoy the daily chores of running a family. You'd know running a family is not the most easy thing to do. To overcome the occasional boredom, pick up a hobby or two.

Tension and irritation are always contagious. If someone in your family is not happy, the gloom will usually permeate everyone. To avoid this problem help your family members to relax. It is always of great help to share the problems of others.

As and when you grow old you'll find that another type of tension is growing on you. This is the tension of growing old.

❋❋❋

But there are ways of coping with this problem too and it is always advisable to age gracefully.

First thing you have to learn as age catches up is to lower the activity-level of daily life. You don't have to perform as much you used to in your younger days. This is natural and there is nothing to feel bad about. Don't expect too much from yourself -- no one else does.

Many people do not know where to put a stop. Everyone needs to retire one day or the other (unless probably you are a politician).

❋ ❋ ❋

There is no definite rule or age for retirement but do it, whenever it suits you, gracefully.

In fact, many people use retirement as a great opportunity to start something afresh. Don't gamble with the money you got from provident fund and gratuity, but take up writing poetry now. Didn't you think all through your life that you could have been a better poet than an insurance agent?

You can even cultivate fresh interests in something which you never thought existed in your domain. What about participating in cultural programmes in your locality? Don't you think that the local club in your area is doing a great job in eradicating illiteracy and it's high time you contributed something?

If you are intelligent and know how to face life, why should you be worrying at all? Remember, life is like taking a bath on a sea-beach. There will be waves, sometimes turbulent, to bother you. Take the waves as they come. Sometimes you dive and let the wave past, sometimes you can rise along with the wave!

When in doubt, pray. Pray to your inner self and gather the strength to face life. A relaxed frame of body and mind helps you to become a complete human being and that is what counts in life.

*** *** ***